Behind These Walls

CORINEA ANDREWS

Order this book online at www.trafford.com
or email orders@trafford.com

Most Trafford titles are also available at major online book retailers.

Printed in the United States of America.

ISBN: 978-1-4269-5324-8 (sc)
ISBN: 978-1-4269-5325-5 (e)

Trafford rev. 01/24/2011

 www.trafford.com

North America & international
toll-free: 1 888 232 4444 (USA & Canada)
phone: 250 383 6864 ♦ fax: 812 355 4082

100 Tons

I carry this boulder along with me
holding my hardships & me on my knees.
I drag it when tired, inch by inch,
this rock of secrets, at me it winks.
Discouragement unhinged by this chain & ball.
My problems are greater than I am tall.
Hoisting this begrudgement when I feel I can't win
is weighing me down, makes me lower my chin.
This punishment bestowed upon my very being,
drains me of life with no chance of fleeing.
Shackled & kept til atonement is done,
I now belong to this 100 tons.

7/13/10

A Push & A Shove

I've asked myself
so many times
Can it change?
Will it all be fine?
Then it occurred
like a slap in the face
Like a thief you stole from me
taking my grace
I gave you my trust
I gave you a chance
It didn't take long
no longer than a glance
You berated me with hands
that once held me with love
You decided to adore me
with a push & a shove
There is no part of me
that deserved what you did
No part of me that isn't safe
unless it can be hidden
With this thorn off my side
I will be strong
You're not entitled
Goodbye, so long

3/20/00

A Smile is a Smile

The world is so much bigger than me.
I'm a speck of dust that can barely be seen.
There's a freedom from being loose from these chains.
The whole picture shows me that I'm actually sane.
I'm not as unique as I once thought I was.
I reflect my memories. Each is just a pause.
I'm not on a pedastal. I'm just a human being
with trials and errors that I need help seeing.
I'm not as alone as I once thought I would be.
These shackles broke open and set me free.
I walk the same path as I see you walk down.
Where a smile is a smile and a frown is a frown.
This is my mind and nothing can rent its space.
When I look at myself, I just see this face.
My eyes are the windows to my open soul.
With acceptance and peace, I filled up the hole.
Despise and despair is now hope and love.
The future in mine to take advantage of.

6/01

ALIVE

If I tell you the truth, will it keep me alive?
If I cry you my tears, will it be the last I cry?
For only a meager part of me tells me I am real
Cast a stone my way so that I can feel
Will you still respect me if I turn away?
Never to look back again, would it be okay?
Pour a cascade of water on me so I may feel clean
Wash me of my blackened wounds so they can't be seen
Lift my head to hold me up, don't just be my shadow
Show me I can do this, the truth may not be shallow
A backward glimpse of time, a step on common ground
With reason to find a way of jumping back on that cloud
The days are slowly closing in as I rest my eyes and mind
To tell the truth to at least myself will keep me much alive

7/6/06

Alone In The Dark

How many more hours?
How many more nights?
Do I have to sit
in the dark full of fright?

How much longer
must I be by myself
watching spiders in webs
creep on old shelves?

Am I going to be alone
for very long?
Will I hide forever
or stay very strong?

When the lights are out
and I hear someone call
should I expect to see shadows
on the walls?

If I hear floorboards creak
in a dark room
should I be prepared
to face my doom?

What if a door should open
when I'm alone
or a stranger keeps calling
all night on the phone?

I will hide in the covers
until dawn breaks
and pray for the morning
when I finally do wake

1986

Amongst the Fittest

You've never lived in my body
You've never explored my mind
Things I have seen as a child
are buried & left behind

My belonging to this universe
is a perception based on self
I'm too little to get down
from on top of this shelf

You'd understand what I mean
if you & I were the same
but I'm the only one in these shoes
who answers to my name

You may not see through my eyes
the way this whole world seems
The shallowness, ignorance, & obliqueness
is much beyond belief

For as far as I've come
& the rainfall I've seen
will keep me real in my daymare
sensing the obscene

With all its lures & traps
amongst the fittest survive
That's why I am who I am
& this is just my life

1/99

ATONEMENT

I'm living with secrets
I've held within
Not heavenly in nature
but filled with much sin
I look for atonement
in every day I live in
Not knowing who I am
or where I've been
All that's been done
is as sharp as a pin
The ice that I skate on
is wearing quite thin
The doors that have shut
When will they open?
From when I left off
Where shall I begin?
From all I have lost
When will I win?
How will I feel safe
When harm is so often?
Do I have the answer?
Is it just I'm not telling?
The holes that have closed
When will they open?
When will my spirit
get rid of the omen?
Please give me freedom
Let me be forgiven

8/06

BETRAYAL

You stole my heart then auctioned it off
to highest bidder, to loudest cough.
You lied to me as you stared in my eyes,
knowing this might be our final good-bye.
You made future plans you didn't expect to keep.
You dug a hole right under me & made sure it was deep.
You wished for me to be fallen so in love with you
just so you could toy with me. I was only one of the few.
You slowly took what I had & then you reached for more.
After you used me to the hilt, you found the one back door.
It took a while to realize, I was the lucky one.
You walked away unfaithfully, weighing me lesser a ton.
I realized once it was over, I deserved more than you gave,
which was everything less than nothing, not even a path to pave.
Now I am free from you. I'm having all the fun.
I've gotten my security back. You left yourself with none.
I saw you yesterday with your new girl-toy.
To you another noone, just a girl-meets-boy.
Her arm around you tightly. Nailed to you, her eyes.
Her hand is in your wallet. You looked like you could die.
For once you are the follower in someone so shallow & grim.
No longer is it he then her. It's knowingly her then him.
I feel I am the successor. I have a life that's new.
You got what you needed - for the screwer to be screwed.

7/7/10

BITTER

He made me feel like a princess,
he held me, he dined me.
I even got flowers,
he danced me, he wined me.
My head got all fuzzy.
I started to stumble.
Into the arms of this man,
I did crumble.
Next thing I knew,
I was lying on the floor.
Not able to move,

my senses no more.
My body was nude.
All feeling was void.
This man who wined me,
fed me some poison.
He did things to me.
He violated my being.
I couldn't even speak.
I couldn't even reason.
I met double faces,
one evil, one wined me.
One captured my heart,
one made me see...
a part of my world,

of my wakings moments.
This nightmare exists,
no sheep, no fence.
It started so innocent,
this man as my date,
then he took me to hell
and made this my fate.
No longer do I enjoy
the fine taste of wine.
It has become bitter,
as had this life.
My Prince Charming
may not have a chance.
Somebody has already
stolen first dance.
I'm much more defensive
where once I held trust.
I leave people behind
coughing in dust.
Caught in the wind
of a tumultuous storm.
Nothing to tear down.
I'm already torn.

6/1/10

Borrowed Time

Living on borrowed hours
Burying time, being a coward
Following not leading
along an open path
Life slipping by
in a lightening flash
Borrowed time
took me away
Not seeing tomorrow
yet stealing today
Pushing me forward
Pulling me back
Getting me ready
for another attack
on myself and others
my pain it does lie
Not being honest
Having no alibi
The hands on the clock
will give a last chime
as I remain here
on borrowed time

3/9/06

BULLY

You're always telling me what to do,
where to go, who to choose.
My mind is not a thing I lack.
I make decisions behind your back.
If we were in school, you'd be the bully.
You push me, then tug at me, as if I'm a pulley.
You can't control yourself so you try to control me.
Like the box on the shelf, you want satisfaction guaranteed.
I can't think for myself. You want the last say.
You pull at my strings like a puppet in a play.
You say what you think with all of your words.
Then you repeat it to make sure you're heard.
When you open your mouth, you tell me what to do
but you won't admit it's the bully in you.
You tell me how to do things as if I am dumb.
You want me to understand I am under your thumb.
What gives you right of the final say?
You're just a child who wants his way.
I have a brain and my own life too.
I will think for myself. I can stand up to you.
Take your opinions, forget your demands.
This is my time and it's not in your hands.

Winter 2009

CAN'T STOP

Like a train on a track, travelling at a great speec
My addiction is swift, on my soul it does feed
Like a car in the fast lane, careening out of contrcl
My living desires created a hole
Like a ship at high sea, sinking to depths below
My faith and conviction had nowhere to go
Like a burning building that feeds on its flames
My will for resistance just never came
Like a ravaging tornado spinning around
The pieces of me are hard to be found
Like a sunami destroys anything near
I just can't stop this addiction I fear
Like a baby dying after its first breaths
My body is telling me it's mourning my death
Like a sinner keeps sinning and feels no remorse
I can't stop the pain that's running its course
Fear and destitution cease my desire to live
Like a thief in the night it takes but won't give
Like the rain pouring down with raging claps of thunder
I cannot stop this spell I am under
God, please help me, as a father lifts his child
Like a caterpillar to a butterfly, I have only a short while

2009

14

CASTING STONES

When you look in the mirror
what reflection comes back?
Do you splinter the wood
in your own little shack?
Do you throw stones
when you live behind glass?
Do fingers point back
in the blame that you cast?
Is credit given
where credit is due?
Analyze me & I'll analyze you.
Is it black & white
in your narrow world?
Is there truth or ignorance
in the words that you hurl?
Is your story one-sided
when it is told?
Do you change scenarios
as the story unfolds?
Is your picture painted
with artificial hues?
Analyze me & I'll analyze you.
Do you look at me
& say my life's oblique?
Does your intolerant mind
think that yours is unique?
Is your acceptance of others
that far from reach?
Do you practice the words
which you insistently preach?
Will you say something's old
when apparently new?

Analyze me & I'll analyze you.
Are others wrong
& you're biasly right?
Is your ire & ignorance
worse than your bite?
Do you horde the truth
when lies spill forth?
Do you stay on track
or fall off course?
Can you face your demons
& see others small truths?
If you analyze me, I'll analyze you.

5/28/07

Child Within

Once again, she's left bruised & broken
before she has a chance to explain the words spoken.
Misguided & lied to one more time
made her stand up & fight for what's right.

One doorway opened as another one shut.
The scars will fade from each & every cut.
She knows what she wants & she knows what she needs.
It's not an open heart that will eternally bleed.

A strong woman has grown from the child within.
She's got places to go & knows where to begin.
Blindness has led her to a dead-end street
but another avenue appeared at her feet.

With shadows behind her, she looked at what lie ahead.
She felt renewed strength to dry tears that were shed.
She brushed off the dirt & reprogrammed her mind.
With much needed self-love, her life will unwind.

With a look in the mirror & a smile on her face,
her wounds will be healing, her steps be retraced.
She's determined to make it & knows that she can
because the child within is now a courageous woman.

Early 2000's

CRINGE

Does it make you jealous
when he looks at me?
Does it make you cringe
when I laugh with glee?
Do you drown in envy
because of my looks?
That I can get your man
without use of hooks?
Is there a war in your head
because I can love?
Because my world is serene
while you push & shove?
Does my intellect intimidate
since you do not think?
Your words come unthought of
without time to blink.
You try to belittle.
You yearn to control
but I have my own mind.
I'm not a doll.
Your vindictive ways
will get you nowhere
because you're nothing to me.
I don't even care.
Manipulation is showing
your fears in your life.
Will he ever marry you
& make you his wife?
Never forget
I will be here forever.
I'm your worst nightmare,
your one & only endeavor.

So take your hostility,
your ridicule & shame
to where the sun doesn't shine.
I'm sick of your games.
You can be your dominating
predictable self
but I've caught on.
I hold the wealth.
If vanity is a sin
I'll still hold my head high.
You can hold him with claws.
Remember, he was first mine.

Early 2000's

Death's Hosts

Death, disease, destruction
is there no way out?
It's everywhere around us
filling us with doubt

Others are being destroyed
as I now do speak
It sneaks upon the restless,
the innocent, the weak

We are gathered here today
to fight this external rage
to cease this end to life
to open up its burly cage

Fatal is the outcome
of this destroyer named disease
The damage is beyond repair
To destruct is its main reason

Lacking in courage and spirit
the meek give their own backs
to be ridden upon by death's own hosts
arriving in wolf-like packs

Future generations
are at an early stake
Our grandchildren, their grandchildren
For all of their sakes

The battle is on heavy
since to us it befell
Death, disease, destruction
Let us fight this hell

10/14/10

Delusionary Mind

You say what you think
whatever's on your mind
not thinking of others
your words are unkind
Not having all facts
you say what you feel
your delusionary mind
is nothing but a shield
You question all things
but when answers are found
you put your feet anywhere
except for the ground
What's up is down
what's wrong is right
you can convince yourself
it's day when it's night
You won't let your guard down
to let anyone in
your availability is
rather quite thin
You won't see others views
there is only one
and that is yours
while others you shun
When will you awake
only to find
that all along it was
your delusionary mind?
Keep facts as facts
unload your gun
opinions are like a**e*
everyone has one

10/14/09

Demon in a Bottle

It stopped me in my tracks again
Making me believe it was my only friend
Like a freight train at a high rate of speed
The crash was so quick, it woke me indeed

Inside is a demon. It comes & it goes
When I invited it in, all the doors closed
Caught in a web of deception & lies
Always having to think up alibis

My friend helps me lie, ruins relationships &
more
It says, "Come. Have a drink with me. I too am
bored."
The blackouts are real. A drunk's not my model
Yet I was convinced I had a friend in a bottle

It moves on because poison spreads around
Now saying to others, "I'm your friend. Sit down."
The many faces it shows, are unique as a
clown's
It says "Come. I'll turn your smile into a frown."

My worst enemy is travelling in a flask
It moved on & where am I?
Where did it leave me last?

2008

Demons Within

At times I feel I'm living in sin
I can't find the door to the cage that I'm in
The windows are shut. The blinds are pulled tight
How do I shine if I won't let in the light?
The battle is rough. The lines are drawn thin
How do I conquer my demons within?
Noone understands my life's been in debt
It's like firing a bullet in Russian roulette
I hide and I run, ending up lost
Where will I find me and what be the cost?
My head's trying to tell me which way to turn
but my body is motionless in a fire that burns
Running amok while my life goes astray
makes me seek solace in an imminent way
My mind, it is tired. My body is weak
My heart, it is breaking. My eyes, they do leak
Searching for something I know is so close
makes me have trust, makes me feel hope
I could sweep up the shards of my broken past
Get courage to look through the one-way glass
I need to believe especially in me
The demons within will then set me free

5/28/07

23

DESTINATION

I came as dust
to this earth
carried in womb
until my birth
Air, land, and sea
all around
To this destination
I am bound
The vastness around me
seems so great
This life I live
will be my fate
All the creatures
here below
know little of all
there is to know
We fend from start
day to day
We learn from what others
have to say
The stars will guide us
The seas will sail
Accomplishments to achieve
Trials to fail
All around me
the space is endless
I'm just a fraction
amongst the rest
So many things
I'll never see
So many things
I'll never be
Born into this life
by choice of another
Added to a family
of sisters and brothers
To be taken with the wind
in one big gust
One day to return
back to the dust

12/30/00

Devil's Lair

Naked and cold
stripped down bare
Living in danger
in Devil's Lair
Tangled in hate
Heavy with lies
Nothing alive
Everything dies
Playing the martyr
yet living in sin
Not digging inside
to see what's within
Being in Hell
my surroundings are red
No comfort or peace
Rage and pain instead
Everyone screaming
"Please let us out!"
Reminders of Heaven
are highly in doubt
A soul caught up
in the flames intense glare
Living for Eternity
in Devil's Lair

3/11/06

Down-Pour

Weaving in & out
Struggling to feel sane
Seeking safe shelter
In a down-pour rain

Needing to see clarity
Behind this false hope
Not able to scream openly
While trying to cope

Knowing all the damage caused
Beyond any repair
Makes it harder to deal with
Makes it harder to share

Can't let go of the past
& can't move ahead
Knowing each day
I have to crawl out of bed

My heart is sore
My mind is aching
I'm tired of the bull**it
& all of the taking

Refusing to give me space
Or fresh air to breath
Smothers me with lunacies
& takes my simple needs

My conviction & expectations
Will help me remain
Whether standing in sunshine
Or a down-pour rain

Summer of '03

F.E.A.R.

F.e.a.r. is fatal, elusive, angry, resentful
Based on self-knowledge, it will cause real distress
Fractions of half-truths dig at your mind
Making you see as can only the blind

Delusions surround you, creating self-doubt
Not knowing the truth when it comes from your mouth
Mixed emotions fill up your heart
& biased opinions can't tell them apart

Weaving in & out of a web of deceit
will without knowledge be doomed to repeat
Damage is done when f.e.a.r. is involved
Nothing is constructive. Nothing is solved

When facts are unknown, you question what's real
When all is in wreckage, what is the appeal?
Salvage your mind. Let go of the doubt
F.e.a.r. holds you hostage & leaves no way out

There is no evidence if something's not real
Appearance is deceiving. Follow what you feel
Hold onto the facts. Don't add your own stuff
You'll soon come to realize when one calls your bluff

Study the realism. Leave no room for f.e.a.r.
In the absence of doubt, the f.e.a.r. will disappear

10/2/09

Fairy Tale

Do you believe in enchantment
& love forever lasting?

Do you find a fairy tale
in every person you are passing?

Kings & queens living
in stone castles in the sky.

A princess taken from her prince,
a lonely tear falls from her eye.

Fighting for love
with a dragon as a player.

Spitting fire during battle
between it & the dragon slayer.

Do you believe in witches
both good & bad,

sharing mystical secrets
& the spells they have had?

Wizards in long cloaks
looking into crystal balls.

Deep dark dungeons
built with thick stone walls.

Look at the world around you
& see the fairy tale unfold.

We can all enjoy a rainbow
even if there is no gold.

Embrace all the beauty
& pass it on to someone else.

You just may be their gypsy queen
with your own fairy tale to tell.

1/00

FALLEN

An angel without wings
I have become fallen
I didn't listen
I didn't hear the calling

I led my life on strings
attached to life-long lessons
I ignored my intuition
I didn't see the blessings

As cold as an icecube
my quality was thawing
I refused to feel the warmth
I continued falling

Like leaves on the trees
I am prone to change colors
with each changing season
I didn't grow with my brothers

With the hand of a giant beast
I was smothered in its' mauling
I gave up my chances
to lift up from where I've fallen

My wings are discolored
and they're covered with scars
I never escaped
I'm still behind bars

All my life was no action
just talking, no walking
Now down on my knees
is where I am crawling

My life has been led
by my meek feeble mind
so many precious things
I've left behind

Now the door's open
Will I still hear the calling
to lift my wings
from where they have fallen?

Mid 2000

THANK YOU, GOD

THANK YOU, GOD
FOR ANOTHER DAY.
THANK YOU, GOD
FOR A PEACEFUL WAY.
THANK YOU FOR GUIDING ME
ON THE RIGHT PATH
TO WALK WITH YOU
TO ENJOY A RAINS' BATH.
THANK YOU FOR THE SUN
THAT BEFALLS MY FACE
AND FOR REACHING OTHERS
IN THIS WORLDS' FAST PACE.
THANK YOU, GOD
FOR THE SEASONS' CHANGE
FOR OPENING UP
THE DOOR TO MY CAGE.
THANK YOU FOR MY FAMILY
WHO PROVE TO ALWAYS BE THERE
TO SHOW ME FORGIVENESS,
UNDERSTANDING AND CARE.
THANK YOU FOR YOUR GIFTS
THAT APPEAR IN WONDROUS VIEW.
THERE ARE NO COINCIDENCES.
I BELIEVE IT IS YOU.

2008

Highway of Life

I'm out on the highway, keeping the speed
Wondering which route my life will lead
I'm searching for exits in case I am lost
Stopping at tolls. Paying the cost.
Life isn't one direction
It's scattered about
Looking for signs
of the inevitable out
Death could be behind me
Travelling in a black car
It might sit right beside me
It might not be far
Each day is one closer
to my ultimate fate
to each moment I'll feel
of love, sorrow, & hate
Red lights that stop me
give me the time
to pull forward cautiously
to stop on a dime
My existance is temporary
on this vast road called life
Taking each day, holding on
with all of my might
Getting into the fast lane
The time just won't wait
Taking every opportunity
before it's too late
I'm sliding my seat back
Hitting cruise control
Relaxing my mind
In touch with my soul
For this life I am grateful
I got it on lend
to do my servitude
Live it up to the end
I take each day as a gift
& its surroundings as ribbons
I put it in park
to unwrap the giving
I'll yield as needed
to play this life's version
This may be
my one-time excursion
I'll dance in the streets
Take this trip with a friend
I may not travel
this same road again

12/2/00

I Believe

I believe that God
has a plan for me
More air to breath
More things to see

He has me here
for only He knows
To see rain & sun
To see little ones grow

The end will come
in only His time
Not giving back
is the only crime

I value myself
& the life I have
To see my face
To hear my laugh

I have many gifts
that are from God
like the gift of language
& the gift of love

I share feelings I have
of grief & joy
I have children to love
a girl & a boy

I have many things
I don't even see
I'm grateful for
what God gave me

7/19/06

I CANNOT...

If I pull back the curtain
what will I see
but a hundred little eyes
staring right through me.
My heart is pounding wildly.
What is it that they want?
I didn't do anything wrong
yet I feel as if I'm caught.
I cannot leave my home.
The sidewalk is too far.
Even if I wanted to,
I couldn't make it to my car.
My head is spinning quickly
and if the telephone rings,
I cannot answer the voice
that telephone may bring.
Paranoid delusions
tell others I'm not sane
but it all seems real to me,
as real as snow and rain.
If someone knocks on my door,
I'll sink into the chair.
Hoping the further I lean into it
will make me disappear.
I know others can see me
right through my very walls
and every voice I hear,
it is to me they call.
I see people turning
to look and glare at me.
I cannot sit on my porch.
I can't face their stare, you see.
Even other rooms
are too far from the one I'm in.
To take a few steps forward
is too much to my chagrin.
Noone can be trusted.

They lie and steal and cheat.
I cannot shake the hand
of anyone I meet.
The doctors try to fix me
with poisons and a wink.
These little pills I am to take,
I toss out down the sink.
Everyone is an enemy.
They talk behind my back.
Pointing fingers, leaning in,
so at me they can laugh.
I close my eyes tightly.
When will they go away?
I try to tell them to get lost.
They don't listen to what I say.
I'm told I am paranoid
but they don't understand.
It's all the accusing statements
and the germs upon their hands.
My world is the real one.
Others invade what's mine.
I know what's going to happen
when the chiming clocks turn nine.
One day, others will see
that I was always right
so staring, knocking, calling my phone,
will go on with the night.
I'll hide under my covers
and wait for the world to sleep.
Even then, it's hard to tell
if in the dark, one leaps.

Winter 2009

it

there's something lingering in the air
above my head, it lays
it's calling to me softly
my skin can feel its' gaze
it stares with capturous eyes
it leaves me spellbound
i am pulled forward
it is me that it has found
a sound is circling around me
when will i feel its' touch?
when will i encounter this being
if it can be called such
a smell of fear tickles my nose
it makes my body shiver
it has made it very clear
it's the taker, i'm the giver
a sliver of moon is in the sky
clouds of fog roll by
everything else stands still
i hear it faintly cry
i take a step forward
sweat climbing my spine
when i reach its destination
what will i find?
i strike out into the emptiness
finding nothing there
i wonder where i am
the answer is "nowhere"
I need to escape
but there's no place to run
heart hammering as i hold my breath
i believe that it has won

1990's

JAIL DANCE

Buzzers ringing
Slamming doors
Tastless food
Hard cement floors
Guards yelling
"Hurry! Stop!"
Green uniforms
Uniformed cops
Tears flowing
down my face
Behind four walls
No preference to race
Only activities
a gym & small yard
Adult day care
Always on guard
No choices to make
Told what to do
Not needing to think
Decisions are few
Looking behind
a one-way mirror
Taking directions
from just one steerer
Asking, then begging
for another chance
Another day living
Another jail dance
Physical exertion
as a slave maker
Handing it over
No givers, no takers
Echos, bright lights

wake up to lock down
Having a smile
turn into a frown
Dirty surfaces
Smell of ammonia
Asking a request
Reply is a "Ha!"
Rude comments
Nasty glares
Soft skin going raw
making me bare
Playing cards
to make time pass
These are the days
I hope aren't my last
Insomnia to hysteria
Depression to glee
Sometimes I just
don't know who to be
Two uniforms, one tote
a towel, a plate
My few belongings
as an inmate
1/2005

JUST WAITING

Deep despair of going nowhere
Noone to talk to of what I must share
Deep secrets still held in this head of mine
Waiting, just waiting, for someone to find.
Why can't I change the suffering within?
Why is it so hard to hold up my chin?
When I try to find peace, why can't I accept
that my mind is trying to give me a rest?
Going about day after day
with robot motions, a mime in a play
Take me deep where I can feel
What's waiting beyond me? What is real?
Sustaining my sanity in this fragile mind
if it seeks shelter from the death-wish I signed
Trying to hold on, keeping a pace
I'm all mixed up in this rat-race
All the despair, all the regrets
Waiting, just waiting
to let out the secrets

Love & Sin

How can I love IT when all seems so wrong.
This very sin I live in, this melancholy song.
I live for the thing that can take me out.
I will surrender to IT, I have no doubt.

IT robs my memory & tears at my soul.
With or without IT, I crawl in a hole.
IT wants all of me; my love, my faith, my pride.
I'm no longer in light, for IT I have lied.
How can I possibly ever win
with these two on my back, my love & my sin?

The feeling is temporary, the obsession forever.
This game is a sickness & IT plays very clever.
To protect my soul & mind is my one & only mission.
I need to drown my vanity in this opposition.
For IT is my lover & I am the sinner
Rolling the dice only proved IT's the winner.

2009

MINDS OF OUR YOUTH

IMPENDING VIOLENCE
INVADING OUR SCHOOLS
USING BOMBS & GUNS
TO PROVE WHO RULES
INNOCENT CHILDREN
BEING TAKEN AWAY
BY OTHERS WHOSE LIVES
HAVE GONE ASTRAY
BROKEN FAMILIES
IN THE AFTERMATH
OF TERRIBLE TRAGEDY
IN WOUNDED WRATH
FACES OF FRIENDS
WHO WILL NEVER BE SEEN
ON THE FRONT NEWS PAGE
ON OTHERS THEY LEAN
SORROW & HEARTBREAK
THESE TEENS MUST FACE
AT THE HANDS OF OTHERS
WITH A CONSCIENCE OF WASTE
THE KILLINGS, THE THREATS
ONE BIG BLOOD-BATH
OF ANYONE IN SOCIETY
WHO STEPS IN THEIR PATH
FEARING THESE CHILDREN
WHILE PROTECTING OUR OWN
AFRAID THAT AT SOME POINT
ONE ENDS UP ALONE
WHERE ARE THEIR MORALS?
WHAT WERE THEIR THOUGHTS?
WHILE TRYING TO PLAY GOD
IT WAS THE DEVIL THEY SOUGHT
SITUATIONS OUT OF HAND
SO MANY THAT WERE KILLED
ALL BECAUSE OF AN IDEA
THAT IT WOULD BE A THRILL
TEARS SPILLED BY OTHERS

WHO LOST SOMEONE CLOSE
TAKEN BY ADOLESCENTS
JUST SO THEY COULD BOAST
THIS WORLD, OUR SOCIETY
IS ONE BIG THREAT
LACKING STRUCTURE IN OUR CHILDREN
THE FUTURE PAYS ITS DEBTS
PLANS OF DESTRUCTION
IN THE MINDS OF OUR YOUTH
WHO SHOW NO GUILT
WHO HAVE NO COUTH
PITY FOR EVERYONE
WHO BECAME INVOLVED
THE KILLERS, THE FAMILIES
& LOVED ONES LOST
ONE DAY REALIZING
WHAT HAS BEEN DONE
ALL AT THE HANDS
OF A BOMB OR A GUN

4/30/99

Moment of Haste

Endless nights
Dreamless sleep
Wanting to fight
a life that's cheap
Daring to stray
but staying put
With prices to pay
Without any loot
Rebelling against time
day after day
Creating a mime
Wanting my say
Drying my eyes
after I weep
these tears I cry
from the life I reap
Lost deep inside
and denying it all
Not wanting to abide
my final call
Twisting, turning,
toward a life of crime
Waiting and learning
Doing my time
Trying to have patience
Trying to find faith
Seeking all that was taken
in a moment of haste
Saying my prayers
behind these walls
Remembering what I had
before my final fall
This is the first day
of the rest of my life
Taking it all
in sorrow and strife
Setting my boundaries
Reaching new goals
Seeing a different light
Saving my soul

5/5/99

My Heart Smiles

All these things I feel inside
I don't know how to explain
I show a smile, shed some tears
on this pillow where my head is laying
I searched my heart. I found a friend
Still these moments are bare
I look for hope. I show a smile
& pray that you're still there
I showed some love. I lent a hand
& had gratitude just for you
I held on with my fingertips
I knew these hours were few
I'll be here if you need me
I hope it always shows
Please look into my eyes
as I promise to never let go
Don't close yourself up to me
& hide behind locked doors
I want to know what you think
These feelings that are yours
What you're sensing down inside
doesn't need to be hidden deep
Some things you may entrust in me
& some you'd rather keep
I want you to know that it hurts
& some things touch me hard
Not thinking things would turn around
from the very start
Maybe there isn't much I can do
but I'm savoring every moment
The time that I have felt loved by you
that's where my heart is spent
It's hard to express emotions
but I know far in my mind
that no matter where I go
you'll always be close behind
It's okay, I want you to know
if you don't feel as I do
I just needed to say today
my heart smiles because of you

11/2009

My Maker: My Taker

With weakened nerves
from the pit of my being
Asking some questions
not given a reason
My heart palpitating
beyond my control
To which I'm not entitled
on opposite end of patrol
I'm crying & shaking
"Who is my maker?
Does anyone want me?
Who is my taker?"
I'm sweating inside
chilled to the bone
Though surrounded by others
I feel so alone
Ahead of my body
my mind races on
Where did I leave it
since it feels gone?
My ears keep ringing
but it's not the phone
Please come & get me
I want to go home

1/2005

Never to be Heard

Tears cried at night that noone will hear
Cringing at sounds because of the fear
Curled up tightly into a ball
To protect thyself, to make the pain dull
Bruises are scattered from here to there
but the mind is the place the scars bare all detail
Emotional, physical, mental despair
Feeling so lonely, as if noone cares
Damaging words affecting my youth
If no other is listening, the point is quite moot
The heartache inside of wanting to be loved
The hurt that I carry when push comes to shove
Hands that should love but are intended for harm
The coldness that's felt instead of the warm
Trying to do the expected for a hug or good word
but the words are unspoken, never to be heard
Afraid to make eye contact due to daily reminder
of the disappointment of knowing nothing kinder
Praying some day to break away free
of what's been robbed at such a great fee
Dear God in Heaven, listen to the moans
in the hearts and voices of those so alone

11/30/00

NEXT TIME

"He didn't do it," she says once again.
"I tripped and fell down," she tells all her friends.
She covers with make-up, the bruise on her eye,
trying not to smudge it with the tears that she cries.
When he says he's sorry, again she believes him,
not realizing her life is on a short limb.
Next time, it's worse. Her hand's in a cast.
"I slammed it in the door," is what she thinks up fast.
He sends her flowers with a sweet little card
saying he'll change, he's just a little marred.
Things go well for a bit. He puts on the charm.
Before she knows it, he's twisting her arm.
"I just bruise easily," she tells mom and dad.
"He's a great guy, the best one I've had."
Next time her friends see her, she's lying in bed,
bandages covering her face and her head.
Doctors say they don't know if she'll awake.
"It was quite a beating her body did take."
He stands at the door, then just walks away.
This time neither of them has anything to say.
The doctors were right, she didn't open her eyes.
She passed in the night and he didn't say good-bye.

2009

No More

I'm moving along now
I've set you free
So, I ask the same of you
to just let me be
Let me be the person
that I like & know
No more intimidation
to make me feel low
No more sleepless nights
where I would turn & toss
I can wear my own clothes
I can be my own boss
I thought I have loved
until I felt hate for the first time
regurgitating inside me
when I could look finally in your eyes
No more hurtful names, pushing, shoving,
no more screaming in my face
My life will go on now
but you I can erase.
All those things you tried
to convinve me that I was
They were all your nightmares
Now you can wake up
You never met the hard-ass in me

too busy being your own
Well, here I am with a PFA
It's time you have been shown
No more threats or vicious looks
I am moving on
Just needed to find
where you've put me
& POOF...
now I'm gone

2008

Oh, Mother of Mine

Oh, mother of mine, where have you been?
Why am I to pay for this terrible sin?
Mother of mine, what have you done?
Like a game of chess, was I just a pawn?

My tiny heart just started to beat
but I'll never get to run with my little feet.
If you heard me cry, would you change your mind?
Don't you want to read me my first nursery rhyme?

My eyes haven't opened but they would've been blue.
If you looked into them, you'd see part of you.
I won't get to hold you or say my first word.
To say "Mommy" or "Daddy" will never be heard.

I'll never push a fire engine or play with a doll.
I'll never get a hug for the times I might fall.
Never pick a flower or climb a tree.
Never see an ant or a bumblebee.

My tiny mouth won't taste a raindrop.
I'll never get kisses or my first lollipop.
I won't see the clouds, weather dark or weather bright,
won't get a puppy or fly my first kite.

I'll not know mum or daddy, or be held in their arms.
Never feel love or protection from harm.
You'll never know if I'm a girl or a boy.
Opportunity will pass to buy me a toy.

I suck on my thumb, my hands are so small,
in which I'll never catch my first bouncing ball.
I'll never feel sun fall upon my face,
not ever hear laughter or eat my first cake.

I'll never hear birds or see green grass.
I'll never have friends or play in a bubblebath.
I won't have my daddy swing me high in the sky.
Oh, mother of mine, why must I die?

Summer of '99

Pergatory

Silence is all around me
yet the deceased yell in my head
telling me things of horror
making it fearful to go to bed

I tell them to be quiet
to find their resting place
When my eyes begin to close
I see each and every face

They want to tell me stories
of their disastrous ends
I try to block them out
but my ears begin to bend

Guilt, hate, jealousy, greed,
Misfortune awaited them all
They refuse to pass beyond
my heads' safe structured walls

Screams so loud they echo
and wails that make me chilled
Feelings of devastation
are not called on by my will

My heart does bleed and cry for them
They are on stifled grounds
Not existing like the rest of us
Just acknowledged for their sounds

The desperation is multiplied
Not one speaks out alone
They tackle all my senses
with each and every moan

I wish for silence always
for them to find their way
Once out of this pergatory
they'll have nothing to say

Mid 2000's

pieces

i'm shattered to pieces
scars are in detail
of an emotional bender
caught in a snare
i look in the mirror
and what do I see?
a stranger of strangers
staring back at me
a blade, a pin
scissors will do
to carve the pieces
of my rendevous
on skin so soft
there are red scars
to show time travelled
alone in the dark
each time i do it
a calmness remains
although just for moments
it helps keep me sane
shattered pieces picked up
from all around
held together by emotions
they are bound
what would i think

if you were me?
a troubled life trampled
in an unstoppable stampede
i hide in the closet
or any small room
to enclose me in comfort
an angelic cocoon
i get out my weapon
whatever's of choice
that's how i do it
to express my own voice
somebody hear me
it happens so fast
my body envelops
into an emotional cast
to free me again
until next time i fail
seeking relief
in a pin or a nail

6/1/10

Poem of an Addict

Feeling incomplete, unloved,
need to fill up your soul?
Why not block out reality
by filling a bowl?
Feeling ashamed & deserted
but it's not your fault?
Just open the wound wider
& fill it with salt.
Cocaine, heroin,
LSD, speed.
What's your drug of choice?
On which do you feed?
Attitude, anger,
but refuse to cry.
Just grab a drink
to choke down that pride.
"Go ahead, just take one.
It won't lead to addiction."
Do you truly believe this?
Fact or fiction?
When you use drugs,
do they become friend or foe?
They took you places
you thought you'd never go.
Jail, institutions,
near-dead, on the street,
helplessness, powerless,
denial, defeat.

Who am I?
Which direction do I turn?
Are these the questions
from which you will learn?
Family, jobs, homes, friends-
these losses can you afford?
Find yourself. Get your life back.
Restitution restored.

2/28/98

POISON IVY

I am Poison Ivy to your skin
a constant *itch to endure
but you still accept my foreverness
it's what your time is for

You keep me under lock and key
inside a velveteen box
The more I said I hated you
is the most you ever got

With pleasure I antagonize you
for a few moments of fun
yet you keep me held hostage
as I respond with a shun

Poison Ivy will grow
around the core of your being
around the black rose I gave you
around one that's now bleeding

Every time you pout and cry
I roll up my blue eyes
because with each new-born hello
comes a blasphemous good-bye

No matter what I do to you
you'll take the whole of me
You want it to be about you
I want it to be about Poison Ivy

5/10

Possessions

I am your glass doll
sat high on a shelf
You've taken all of me
left me with no self
You take me down often
whenever it is handy
You use me for a night
use me as "arm candy"
You dress me up
and you can take me out
You feel that without me
you'd lose all your clout
I'm a flower in your garden
growing just for you
Possessions placed in a vase
once picked, won't grow beyond you
Eventually, once again
you'll put me back on the shelf
collecting wispy webs of white
losing time all by myself
Beauty is only skin deep

it will age, wither, and wear

No longer the chosen one

she's pretty with long hair

Forever since taken out

to be your "showroom" girl

I went from being a diamond

to a smaller yellowed pearl

Separated from each other

yet don't know who to be

This possession you once "took down"

is now just a boring memory.

5/2010

Power of ENVY

Don't let it leer up
& show on your face
FEAR & JEALOUSY
is not part of GRACE
Your eyes are green
although, actually blue
What you're in ENVY of
you haven't a clue
Is it the big house?
A red sportscar in the garage?
What about PRESTIGE & POWER?
A job in corporate law?
Do you make your own rules
ignoring all flaws?
Is it the wife & two kids,
the dog & the cat?
You can't paint the fence white
or wear the black top hat
The mask you are wearing
is a green-eyed creature
RESENTMENT & JEALOUSY
in each wrinkled feature
You express ill-will
on those who have much
They seem to take in
whatever they touch
Appearances & facades
can look so deceiving
Your side of the street

may just need a cleaning
The power of ENVY
can make a man weak
Can strip away morals
& mess with the meek
Noone knows what goes on
behind closed doors
In JOY, LOVE & SECURITY
they may be poor
Smiling in the community
yet concealing their flaws
If you blinked even once
you may find it's a mirage
If you have all your senses
sight, sound, touch & smell
Take them as the treasures
unto which you befell
Be gracious & tolerant
Share what you can
You'll find out these aptitudes
make you a very rich man

Middle 2000's

Queen of Hearts

Fighting & Reliving
My One True Defense
Not Knowing Which Side
I'll Fall Off the Fence
Survival & Struggle
Are My Two Techniques
of Getting Within
the Things I Can Reach
This World is One Chapter
in a Great Big Book
Showing Me the Grander Picture
Just Look
Despair I Have Felt
in This Card Game of Life
Handing Me Cards at Random
No Choices, Just Strife
Ace of Spades
Queen of Hearts
Only One Card
Keeps Them Apart
There Are No Coincidences
in How the Cards Fall
Just Keep on Answering
Each & Every Call
I Won't Miss Out
on This Big Adventure
Each Step & Chapter
Takes Me on Further
I'll Struggle & Fight
For What it is Worth
in Each New Day
A Beautiful Rebirth

Early 2000's

Rage

Chemical thoughts leak through his brain.
It makes him unsound, it makes him insane.
With words screamed at noone in an empty room,
the rage inside will not end soon.
Holes in the walls and a broken door,
pieces of glass lay on the floor.
His face is red from all the heat,
looking for someone or anything to beat.
He can't calm down except from exhaust.
His life is shortened, each special moment lost.
Savoring pain inside and out
is what he feels it's all about.
Not letting go to get some peace,
will find him short on his life's lease.
He's battling hostility and rage within,
resentments caged up against his sins.
The violence is unspeakable, he hears his head pound.
Bright rushing red is the only sound.
The chairs are upturned, he sits on the floor.
Exhausting himself, he gives nothing more.
Not recognizing wrongness in each of his acts,
he's doomed to repeat most of his past.
His body now rests, confused with the change.
not realizing the silence just isn't the same.
Next time around, is likely to be worse.
Can he afford it? It isn't his first.
He can pick up the pieces of his broken past.
Just like the mirror, just like the glass.
Without help and release from the anger and pain,
his life is on hold. Time is ticking away.
Never again can he reclaim time lost.
He'll pay admission for his act of sloth.
He can play director up on his stage
but the curtain may close with his final rage.

Winter 2009

RECYCLABLE SOUL

At one time, maybe I was a medievil princess
who lived in a castle of stone
where others there died before me
in a dungeon lies their bones.
I may have left the earth by suicide
since I couldn't betroth the one I chose.
The poison that I swallowed
placed me in a fatal doze.

I could've been an indian
riding my horse across the plains,
sleeping in animal-hide teepees
in bouts of torrential rains.
One day,as my headdress feathers
blew in the faint warm breeze,
I was pierced with a leaden bullet
and died with the greatest of ease.

I may have been a slave
my skin as black as ash.
Rapes and beatings were a part of my life-
for my work, never seeing cash.
Little did I know as the straps cut in,
my heart would begin to grow weak.
Just one day I decided to give up
and my heart took its very last beat.

I might have been a housewife
with several children and a drunken spouse.
I wasn't allowed to speak or look at him.
I was as timid as a mouse.
One day, he couldn't control his rage
and his hands began to clench.
I died at those hands that once held me with love.
Noone has seen me since.

Today, I am a young mother
and again I am heavy with child.
Going through life at different times
withered, exhilerated or wild.
I'm still walking with all the others
just playing out my role,
soon to be dust in the wind again
trading in my recycable soul.

2/23/02

RUNAWAY

She's a teenage runaway
with misshapen memories to hide
She left her home and family
Went and hitched a ride
The backpack that she left with
holds a few keepsakes
Some stuff that she can look at
on every day she wakes
Pictures of her brother,
a diary and small bear
a letter from her best friend
with an ink spot and a tear
The letter reminds her of good times
of summer and her friends
The diary is from long ago
which soon came to an end
The bear is from the crib
that once held her baby frame
The picture of her brother
was before he had a name
She wears the same old clothing
she threw upon her back
Her sneakers have small holes in them
Her shelter is a shack
She hustles on the streets
just for a cup of soup
She comforts in a city block
with those she calls The Group
Burden of being a daughter and sister
with expected morals as firm as stone
was too much to live up to
Much better to be alone
She'll walk each block with tired legs
on feet in dirty shoes
to catch up with her trespasses
and find out her own truth
Home is far behind her
with no plans of going back
She's got a photo, letter and stuffed bear
in a little pack

7/6/10

SEVEN

I AM SEVEN
I COME TO YOUR DOOR
YOU WON'T BE EXPECTING ME
I COME ON LIKE A WAR
SIN SPINS ALL AROUND ME
LIKE FIRE IT DOES SPREAD
TAKING LIVES IN AN UNRULY STORM
THEN SHELTERING ITS' DEAD
TAKING AS MANY AS I CAN
EATING THEM TO THE BONE
THERE ARE SEVEN OF ME
I SEE YOU'RE ALL ALONE
IF SORES BREAK OUT UPON YOUR SKIN
SEEPING & FULL OF PAIN
I WILL BE THE SALT WATER IN THEM
FOLLOWED BY TORRENTIAL RAINS
THE SHEDDING OF BLOOD SHOULD SHOW
HOW SERIOUS I AM
I AM A DRAGON. I AM A BEAST
STOP ME IF YOU CAN
YOU'LL HEAR THE SCREECHING UP ABOVE
THEN BE SEERED BY AN INTENSE BURN
DARKNESS WILL ENVELOP ALL AROUND
& YOU'LL HAVE NOWHERE TO TURN
COUNT ME.......
ONE, TWO, THREE, FOUR, FIVE, SIX, SEVEN
I AM RADICALLY
DIFFERENT THAN HEAVEN
BUT IF YOU HAVE ATONED

MEETING THE END WITH GRACE
IF YOU CAN STARE ME
RIGHT IN THE FACE
DISEASE, SPILLED BLOOD
DARKNESS, FIRE
DEMONS, FIERCE STORMS
SCREAMS AFTER SILENCE
WILL NOT SHOW UP AT YOUR DOOR
WILL NOT TRACK YOU DOWN
YOU'RE FREE TO GO
YOU'VE BEEN UNBOUND
BUT IF YOU CHOOSE SIN
& HELL OVER HEAVEN
IT'S NICE TO MEET YOU
I AM SEVEN

10/14/10

STOLEN MEMORIES

IMAGES PASSING THROUGH MY MIND
OF TIMES THAT DIDN'T SURVIVE
I CLOSE MY EYES TO DREAM AGAIN
TRYING TO HELP THEM STAY ALIVE

THE SECRETS OF STOLEN MEMORIES
AND WHAT IT HAS DONE TO MY SOUL
THE SACREDNESS THAT I MUST HIDE
HAS REALLY TAKEN ITS' TOLL

THE BITTER-SWEET ILLUSIONS
REMAIN HELD TO MY SIDE
THE IMPRESSION OF LIFES' SECURITY
WILL NO LONGER BE MY GUIDE

I'M DECIEVED BY ALL THESE PASSAGES
THAT TRY TO LEAD ME ASTRAY
WHO ELSE WILL SUFFER THE COST
IF I DON'T FIND MY WAY?

MY LIQUID DREAMS GO IN
COME OUT
I THEN OPEN MY EYES
TO MY WHEREABOUTS

I WILL REMAIN STEADY AND FIRM
ON MY BELIEFS
NOONE CAN TAKE THEM
NOT A CLEVER THIEF

SHUTTING DOWN, THE DAY IS DONE
I MUST RESERVE MY TIME
UNTIL THESE STOLEN MEMORIES
AGAIN COME VISITING MY MIND

1990's

Suffering Yesterday
Surviving Today

Innocence lost
gone astray
Suffering yesterday
surviving today
Stolen memories
from the past
Tied up forever
in wasted wrath
Nothing forgotten
bound in rope
Losing ground
losing hope
Hidden feelings
hidden tears
Growing up
in times of fear
Childhood taken
a grown-up too soon
Trying to break free
of this cocoon
Noone to turn to
nowhere to run
Where to find trust
when guilt weighs a ton
Anger, aggression
indignation, resent
How to let go
when I want to repent
Where is the solitude?
Where is my peace?
Where is my seclusion

when I just want to scream?
Confusion and frustration
over the question "Why?"
Wanting to live
while I'm dying inside
Seeking relief from distress
to show me the way
Suffering yesterday
surviving today

3/98

SWALLOWED

I'm afraid for myself & what comes from within
At times I'm a covered angel living with guilt & sin
I try to block out. I try to shelter within
I'm unaware of myself. I'm feeling close to nothing
I'm trying to escape from the hurt lying inside
My heart strings are pulled. My mind can tell me lies
I need to find the power. I need to find the strength
to jump from this high tower & hope for enough rope length
I need to stay solid, stay grounded in this goal
I won't let this swallow me down a gaping hole
I may be a little shattered. I may be hopelessly confused
but it fares better than lost & crazy, being accosted & abused
Unless an invisible force carries it off in the breeze
nothing short of a miracle can take these weights off me

late 90's

Sweet Misery

On my tongue like acid rain
Makes my composure hard to regain
The taste of sweet misery is coming within
My veins, its tunnel; its hell, my sin
It has me under lock & key
but I wouldn't want to be free
I feel it capture all that I am
Drowning until it breaks open the dam
It's me & you, & we both agreed
I signed a contract, you laughed with glee
I stay afloat but on my knees
to rise again for sweet misery
It can have all of me. I want nothing but it
It can have everything. Every last bit
Each drop of poison is my enemy
yet I say "Please" to sweet misery

8/30/10

The Taking

My dreams come to life
while in deep sleep
My masterful mind
cringes at screams
My body trembles
because I know what's next
What comes from my subconsious
is worse than a hex
A child under water
eyes looking at me helplessly
While I try to tug him free
a branch holds him selfishly
Night sweats, night terrors
won't allow me to waken
Not right now, not until
I'm there for the taking
Running, feet pounding
but I'm getting nowhere
It's catching up quickly
soon my worst nightmare
In my dreams of the night
are those that love me
Soon to realize
that they're only my enemies
Haunting faces, taunting words
come from their lips
With sharp gnashing teeth,
at my limbs they begin to rip
Powerful people in control
with bodies so strong
grip me tightly with pain
eerily singing a song
Blood spills in pools
running under my feet
They're frozen in place
so sticky from heat
Darkness upon me
until I awaken
For now there's no light
I'm there for the taking

3/99

The Woman I Am

Carrying chains
Weight of cement on my feet
Trying to drag onward
although I feel beat
Falling in deeper
to my own man-made hole
Trying to break away
from behind these walls
Where is she?
The woman I was to be?
How did I lose her?
What will set her free?
Held down by burdens
with heavy debts to pay
I let her hide away slowly
A little bit each day
She was to be that
She was to be this
but I let her drown slowly
in my own shallow abyss
Like a ghost from my past
I'm now trying to catch her
Her living light lingers
if I run up behind her
If I can grasp on
to the woman I was
the woman I became
will become half-doth
The light will get brighter
if I keep it aflame
The woman I am
will finally own her name
If I know who she is
and where she's come from
the woman I am
will be the one I've become

1/4/10

TOUGH

While Daddy's away, Momma's frolicking in bed.

Except she's not with Daddy. It's another man instead.

I can hear the giggling, the sighs, and the moans,

as I sit in dirty clothes, hungry and alone.

Momma doesn't want more kids, she says I am enough.

When I tell her I am cold and lonely, her single reply is "Tough."

I ask her in a quiet voice what made her heart so torn.

She looks at me and says it happened the day that I was born.

I wish that I could disappear but I have nowhere to go.

Momma, Daddy, and these strange men are the only people I know.

I have no playmates and my only toy is a stuffed doll.

I hold onto her tightly as I slide down against the wall.

Tears stream down my face and fall upon my shirt.

I have nothing on my little feet except a lot of dirt.

The stranger and my mommy emerge from the back room.

He hands her cash quickly. Daddy will be home soon.

Momma leans down to me. I smell alcohol on her breath.

She tells me not to say a word or it may cause my death.

When Daddy comes home from work, Momma shows no sorrow.

All will be forgotten, at least until tomorrow.

2008

Trap

My body is numb
brain sharp as a tack
I'm trapped in my body
there's no turning back
Lost control of movement
a few years ago
Now I sit in this chair
with disease as my foe
Somebody to feed me
dress me and wash me
I can do none of these
things placed upon me
I wait for each day
to get closer to the last
Every day in the future
is further from my past
I think of my children
whom I'll leave behind
in a world so hasty
with blind leading the blind
What is beyond here?
I'm so close to see
Where once again I'll dance
in my body so free
My lungs will stop working
no longer of access
My eyes will shutter
This breathing's my last
I'll smile at loved ones
I've patiently waited
for the pain to cease
in this trap that I've hated
6/1/10

True Colors

Why can't people be themselves?
Just what holds us back?
We're human beings with basic needs
It's honesty that we lack
Everyone thinks it's an emerald world
but where are all the jewels?
Everything has to be such a fight
When can we end this duel?
We see the look in others eyes
Their thoughts are green with envy
Why do they try to play out life?
Who are they supposed to be?
We live in a world that's black and white
'They' say society rules
but who says we have to listen
to this universe of obstinate fools?
Their lives are held by standards
Their morals are set in gold
They all pass their judgement
and do as they are told
Some have hearts of red
Others hearts of stone
Challenge those to show their true colors
"Show us your true-blue bones."

Early 1990's

Twilite

After midnight, when I can't sleep
Way past counting whooly sheep
I lay and think while in my bed
of countless obsessions in my head
Is the door locked? Are any lights on?
Is the stove off? Is it almost dawn?
I wish the doctor would prescribe for me
something so floating dreams I'll see
Dreams of stardust and candy canes
Pictures of going down memory lane
Instead, I lay here in the twilite
knowing my growl is worse than my bite
I go anywhere that dreams don't come soon
No seeing the runaway dish with the spoon
Are the windows locked? Did I turn off the stove?
These hours I toss, I'm beginning to loathe
Doc, give me something to fight the committee in my head
I'm no Goldilocks too big for bears' bed
I need pleasant dreams that make my head swoon
Give me my cow to jump over the moon

8/29/10

When Two Worlds Collide

The masks we wear to hide the faces
don't cover much. It's all an oasis.
We grin & bare what we must endure.
We laugh & scoff whenever unsure.
The triumphs we achieve can't get us through.
It falls apart without use of glue.
Euphereal colors adorn our earth.
Valued by all for less than its worth.
Much taken for granted while we act out a lie.
The enexpected road ahead will travel on time.
Our lives are a mystery for us to unfold.
A precious gift for strong arms to hold.
Uncover the veil. Don't outlive a lie.
The day will come when our two worlds collide.

10/3/00

Who I Am

Silence is flowing like ripples on a stream.
Emptiness is around me. My mind feels so serene.
No matter what others say, I know how far I've come.
I know who I am, where I've been and what I've done.
Willing to accept this, I put a foot in front of the other.
As I begin walking, I begin to shed my cover.
I will bare my spirit for anyone to see.
Don't care what they think. At least I'm being ME.
My life isn't a game for others to play.
I will live it the way I want it portrayed.
I'll deal with the consequences of all of my actions.
In a mathematical equation, it's just a small fraction.
In the whole scheme of things, if you're still confused
don't live vicariously through me. Find someone else to use.
Film your own soap opera. Let me live my own.
Then hit fast forward and leave me alone.

Early 2000's

Will Power

I can ask for frgiveness
& to be shown the way
but God's will be done
unto taday.
I can ask for patience
& a little love too.
I can request some guidance
just for me & you.
I can't manage myself,
not on my own.
If I just trust in God,
I'm never alone.
I don't need to know
each twist & turn.
Through my mistakes
is how I must learn.
As one of God's children,
I'm not here to be hurt
but to enjoy my time clean,
I must dwell in some dirt.
He knows what's best
when it comes to my life,
when I must bow down,
when I should fight.
Help me remember,
I can't have my way.
God's will be done
unto today.

8/30/06